Pouring Out God's Grace

from a Mason Jar

Other books by Willie E. Burge/Robinson:

Mama's Church Hattitude

Pouring Out God's Grace

from a Mason Jar

WILLIE E. BURGE/ROBINSON

RADIANT HEART PRESS
An imprint of HenschelHAUS Publishing, Inc.
Milwaukee, Wisconsin

Images from public domain or family collection.

Published by
Radiant Heart Press
An imprint of HenschelHAUS Publishing, Inc.
Milwaukee, Wisconsin
www.henschelHAUSbooks.com

ISBN: 978159598-823-2
LCCN: 2021931997

Printed in the United States of America.

I want to dedicate this book to my mother,
Zennie Burge, whose unfailing love and spiritual
guidance has been my anchor and a guiding light;
my deceased father, Albert Burge;
my sister Pearl, my encourager and
prayer partner in my spiritual walk;
my sister Sadie, who always has a listening ear;
and the fond memory of Alvin,
who encouraged me to continue writing (deceased).

Special thanks go out to my sister in Christ,
Arrila Eversley, my Tuesday Bible Class,
my cousin Nate for his wonderful photos,
and sister in Christ who insists on being unnamed.

Table of Contents

Chapter 4

Flowers Among the Rocks

Chapter 5

The Fragrance of Praise

Chapter 6

God Orchestrates Events to Fit His Plan

Chapter 7
Faith Moves the Soul Beyond
What the Eyes Can See

Chapter 8
A Smile from Heaven

Preface

*T*his book was written to encourage, inspire, and to invite each reader to look beyond life's circumstances through the lens of faith to see God's hand of grace pouring out upon our lives daily.

I encourage you to allow God to speak to you on your life's journey. As you read these true stories, testimonies, reflections, and Scriptures, it is my prayer you will clearly see that God's grace transcends our struggles as we approach His throne room in our time of need.

The Mason jar is a metaphor to show how God's grace is not contained but poured out daily. For example, as you will read, He used the hands of a six-year-old girl to pour out His favor on her mother, who had fainted. The water represents an act of obedience.

"There is work you must do, so get busy
and pour out to others as I pour into you."

Introduction

*T*he little girl was playing in an open field by the creek, chasing butterflies and occasionally stopping to pick wildflowers, placing them in her Mason jars. Her giggles pierced the air and reached the ears of her mother, sitting on the bank of the creek.

Mom looked over her shoulder to check on her daughter and grinned as she watched the little one dance across the field, braids flowing in the air as the wind captivated her daughter's unleashed spirit.

Suddenly Mom felt a tug on her fishing line as the bobber disappeared under the water. Reeling in, she smiled as she caught the large white bass attached to the hook. She placed it in a small bucket and hummed her favorite song, *Amazing Grace*, reflecting on God's grace in giving her such a beautiful child.

From the day her daughter was born, Mom could see God's favor on her baby, and she realized He had a special purpose for her life. Feeling like Hannah, the mother of Samuel, she made a similar vow to dedicate her own child's life to God by giving her girl back to Him.

She felt her daughter had a spiritual flame that would draw others to Christ.

A big smile came over her face. *Ahh*, she thought, *that's why I named her Pearl, like a precious jewel. She will be like the oyster story*: The oyster found the sand to be an annoyance, and it thought, "If I can't remove it, I will improve it." So the grain of sand turned into a pearl. And so her daughter's story would go. Pearl would have many challenges in life, each one allowing her to grow stronger in her faith in God.

All of a sudden, Mom felt faint. She called softly to Pearl, saying, "Mama needs you to go down to the creek and get her some water."

In that instant, God took control. He caught Pearl by the hand and guided her feet down the slope. By

His grace, she dipped her Mason jar into the water, raced back, and poured it on her mother's face.

Opening her eyes, Mom thanked God first and then praised Pearl for a job well done. Mom thought, *What a fish story I'll have to tell years from now*. And since that day, God's saving grace had been her guiding light.

Years later, she could see God preparing Pearl for His divine purpose, using her to pour into the lives of others.

That day on the bank of that little creek in the Deep South, God said, "This is the vessel I've been hoping to find. I'll mend it and use it and make it Mine. I need this plain earthly vessel that I can fill with My power and might."

So that day He took Pearl's heart and molded and shaped it in His own way and said to her, "There is work you must do, so get busy and pour out to others as I pour into you."

Chapter 1
Wordless Groans,
Powerful Intercessions

The Teacher's Test

Students arriving early for school had to report to the cafeteria and remain there until the start of the school day. Before being allowed to enter, they were required to show their student IDs.

One morning, while standing at my post, a student walked past me without stopping to show his ID. I politely said, "Young man, I need to see your

ID." He became belligerent and verbally threatening. It was alarming because I didn't usually encounter this type of behavior. I didn't recognize him and only knew he was an upperclassman.

I usually wrote up the disruptive ones right away, but other students were coming in, so I made a mental note to handle it later

A few days after that incident, I took time off because my sister was having back surgery. On April 20, 1999, I was sitting in the hospital waiting room grading papers while I waited for my sister to return from surgery. The TV was on, and the program was interrupted by a reporter who said, "We have breaking news regarding a shooting at Columbine High School in Littleton, Colorado. We know there are some casualties."

As I listened, a chill went down my spine. While details unfolded, I had a flashback to the incident with the student at my school. My thoughts were interrupted by a nurse calling my name to let me know my sister was on her way back to her room.

As my attention shifted back to my sister, God spoke to me in a still, quiet voice, saying, "Leave that incident with the student at your school to Me." Psalm 46:10 immediately came to my mind, which states, "Be still and know that I am God." As I meditated on those words, I was able to assist the nurse with the care of my sister. I realized God had carried me into His private sanctuary because I felt the power and presence of the Holy Spirit.

When I returned to school, the previous week's incident with the student was only a distant memory. My focus was back on my students. I picked up my keys and proceeded to empty my mailbox. Back in my classroom, I sorted my mail to see what I needed to respond to immediately. There was a handwritten note that caught my attention. It simply said, "Teacher, I apologize for my behavior toward you the other day."

I sat down and reflected on the note for a minute. I realized that the student didn't know my name and I didn't know his, but God did. When I prayerfully gave it to Him, He had already worked it out. Even though there was no date on the note, I believe it was written the moment I gave that concern to God.

In my sister's hospital room, God knew I needed to focus on the now.

He asks us to trust Him today for the provisions of tomorrow, which He has already made.

The lesson I learned from that incident is that we should not focus on who is against us but trust God as we walk by faith, not by sight. Romans 8:31 says it all: "What then shall we say to these things? If God is for us, who *can be* against us?"

Bullies Will Pay

Blessed are they whose iniquities are forgiven
and whose sins are covered.
Romans 4:7

I heard a man speak to a group of students about his life story. He mentioned how he loved to bully students he thought were weak and would not fight back. He said he remembered this one particular male student who wore large, bifocal glasses. Each day, he would seek out the other student, call him "Four Eyes," push him down, and laugh at him. This bullied student was smart and always knew the answers to all of the class questions.

The speaker stated that he dropped out of school, lived a life of crime, and became "the most powerful drug dealer in his state," which made him wanted by the police. He had always managed to stay one step ahead, but then one day when he let his guard down, he was caught and thrown in jail with no bail. As he sat in his cell, his life flashed before him. Thinking he would spend the rest of his life in prison, he lost all hope of ever being free.

On the day of his trial when he walked into the courtroom, his heart sank because the judge was "Old Four Eyes." From the look on the his face, the judge recognized the troublemaker from school and remembered how he used to taunt the boy, push him down, and hurl insults at him. The judge gave the troublemaker the maximum prison term.

We, too, were sinful bullies with no regard for the Word of God. It was Jesus who bore our sins on Calvary's cross, for we were locked in the prison of our own sins. Jesus gave His life to unlock our prison doors by shedding His own blood and setting us free. Jesus, the Righteous Judge, is the only one who can free us from the prison of sin.

Springtime—Seed Time—Newness and Freshness

To everything there is a season.
Ecclesiastes 3:1

God designed the four seasons to be distinctly different, and they all work together to bring life and growth. This is true for nature and in our personal lives.

You might be in your spring season where there has been a new diagnosis, as in the case of a young girl from my church. I remember her excitement after graduation. She looked forward to attending college.

After completing her freshman year, she received the diagnosis of having two brain tumors. When surgery was performed, only one of the tumors could be removed. Rather than being in a season of despair, she was always in a season of gratefulness, because she has been planted in the Word of God.

One might ask how she became so strong in her faith at such an early age. The seeds of her faith were first planted by her mother, who used Proverbs 22:6 as her guide: "Train up a child in the way he should go." Her mother's faith came through 2 Timothy 1:5:

"When I call to remembrance the genuine faith that is in you, which dwelt first in your grandmother Lois and your mother Eunice, and I am persuaded is in you also."

This young girl's spiritual growth will continue to take place as she goes through her seasons and as they work together to bring about God's perfect plan for her life.

Prayer

Rejoice in the Lord always.
Again, I will say, rejoice!
Philippians 4:4

Lord, help me to rejoice in the midst of my season of adversity; I will keep my eyes on You as I study Your Word, realizing that my joy is not based on the circumstances around me but is the result of Your presence within me. Let my life's seasons be a testimony of Your faithfulness.

Chapter 2
God Will Have the Last Word

So, Sarah died in Kirjath Arba (that is,
Hebron) in the land of Canaan,
and Abraham came to mourn for Sarah
and to weep for her.
Genesis 23:2

Journey of Testing

Reflecting on this scripture, I thought about the words to the song, *I Cried My Last Tear Yesterday*. It had been only a few days since my aunt's home-going service. There was an emptiness that can't be explained. She had been a part of my life since birth. She was like a mother, sister (at times), and best friend.

I found myself in the darkness of God's divine providence, but I had comfort knowing that "weeping may endure for a night, but joy comes in the morning" (Psalms 30:5). The voice of Solomon spoke to me from Ecclesiastes 3:4, reminding me there is "a time to weep, and a time to laugh; a time to mourn, and a time to dance." I received those words in my wounded spirit and allowed them to begin the process of healing.

My husband, his brother, and I packed our clothes and started out on our journey. Our plans were to travel to my hometown where I would visit my family, and after a few days, they would continue to Houston, Texas. There, they would visit friends and relatives and take care of their mom's gravesite (the main purpose for the trip).

Our trip to Mississippi was peaceful. There was no rush to get to our destination. In fact, I remember at one of our rest stops my husband enjoyed watching the squirrels chasing each other through the patches of wildflowers, which seemed to be arranged by God Himself. We allowed God to teach us about His creation and see His character traits. We embraced

Philippians 4:6, not to be anxious about anything, but in everything give thanks.

God was in control of our journey. He never lays out a road map but simply gives us markers along the way, pointing to Him. God allows us to travel the journey one step at a time, providing a light for our path. He doesn't give blazing illumination, but just enough for our next step.

When we arrived at my parents' home, my husband and his brother went fishing. They caught several fish and stated that upon their return from Texas, they were going to catch the big one.

After visiting for a couple of days, my husband and his brother left for the next phase of their journey to Texas. My sister and I trailed them to the interstate and waved goodbye. Looking back, I now realize God gave us peace on the trip from Milwaukee to prepare me for my journey ahead. God's preparation is always His preservation.

Thursday, July 17, 1997, day started out great. My sister and I went shopping and ran into a cousin I had not seen in years. We had a good reunion.

My most cherished visit was with my best friend, Clara. Our visits were always special. This one seemed to have a greater significance. Our bond of friendship was that of kindred spirits, perhaps because we share the same birthday and temperament.

I found out that my friend Bertha, who lives in Los Angeles, was in town. We made plans to meet. I was looking forward to that visit since we had not seen each other since high school.

That reunion never took place. The day before our scheduled meeting, I was awakened in the early morning by the ringing of the phone. My niece in Milwaukee was on the other end screaming hysterically, "Aunt Willie, Uncle Willie is in the hospital in a coma!"

My husband, in a coma? This was too much to process. The next few hours became a blur of tears, confusion, and mental numbness.

I was caught up in a living nightmare. My vacation plans came crashing down into a million pieces.

God's Spiritual Markers

On any journey, there are stops along the way. On this one, God had provided markers at every stop, pointing me to Him through other people.

Marker One

God had my best friend in place. When I called to tell her about my husband, she said, "You pack and I will call the airlines." She came to pick me up, since the airport is ninety miles away.

As I sat in my window seat on the plane, I noticed the man in the aisle seat was talking to a child across the aisle. Realizing the child was the man's son, I indicated I would exchange seats so they could sit next to each other. As I switched seats and tried to hold back tears, the dad thanked me. I remember hearing the little boy ask his father, "Why is the nice lady crying?"

He couldn't imagine how my heart was breaking. There were so many questions and no answers. God gives us time in the wilderness to provide refreshment for our troubled souls. And when we least expect it, His answers come in many ways.

When I changed planes, I had a layover, and the exact place I sat down had been prepared by God to provide answers to some of my questions. A man rolled a lady in a wheelchair to a spot next to my seat. I really wasn't aware of her presence because so many thoughts were racing through my mind. *Is he in pain? He's all alone*, my spirit cried to God. My turmoil was interrupted when the lady in the wheelchair asked, "Where are you going?"

There was so much relief to talk about my ordeal. I told her that my main concern was the standard of care my husband was receiving because I didn't know anything about the hospital he was in.

She said, "I can assure you that he is in the best hospital in Houston. I know because I have been in that hospital many times."

At that moment, I could feel God's peace. Although the storm of anxiety was still raging, His peace allowed me to focus on Him.

Another Marker—Angel Nurse

> *Do not forget to entertain strangers,*
> *for thereby some have entertained*
> *angels unaware.*
> Hebrews 13:2

When I arrived at Herman Hospital, I was directed to go to the ICU. Entering the room, I could see my husband hooked up to several monitors and he was having seizures. I asked the attending nurse to please give him something to stop them. I was amazed at how quickly those seizures stopped after she gave him an injection.

There was something so angelic about her presence. Her essence had a spiritual component around which her spirit revolved, a power that flowed from a higher being. The compassion and care she gave my husband seemed to come from a spiritual energy that emanated from God, consistent with His character.

She performed her duties as if she were serving the Creator with her total being, operating within the boundaries of divine truth (Matthew 2:37). And she had so much patience with me. She taught me how to read the monitors and participate in some of his care.

When I look back on that day, I can see how quickly the seizures stopped upon my arrival. I can see how God spoke from Isaiah 65:24, "Before they call, I will answer; and while they are yet speaking, I will hear."

One More Marker—My Sister Arrived

God sent my sister at the right time. I remember my sister crying when I left for Houston. I told her to remain home and come at a later date. God had to prepare her to support me with her spirit, not her tears. She told me she would not cry.

Fourteen years later, we talked about her promise not to cry. She stated, "No, I never allowed you to see me cry. God prepared an empty room nearby just for me, and when the most difficult times came, as I watched your husband struggle and saw your sorrow, I would steal away to that empty room. There, I would jump up and down and wave my arms and cry as loud as I wanted to."

You have to know my sister. She can tell things with so much humor, one can picture her in that empty room.

She said, "Sometimes I would jump so high I would clear the floor."

I thank God for my sister. When she came, she became my eyes, ears, and feet. It is amazing how God can bring you through the most difficult situations and you can look back and find humor.

Final Marker—God's Final Preparation

First Preparation: The first visit was from my husband's cousin and his wife, whom I had never personally met. Immediately his wife said to me, "I love you." From there, a special bond formed. God sends His spirit of encouragement through family and friends.

Monday, July 21, 1997, 4:00 in the morning, God was preparing me to stand, as there was nothing left to do. My husband's temperature was extremely high, and his blood pressure was rising. I was sitting by his bed crying and praying. Suddenly, I felt a dark cloud all around me. In that cloud, I could feel God's presence.

My physical strength was gone, but I felt strength in His presence. I couldn't eat or sleep, despite friends and family encouraging me to drink water and try to eat something. I know how Elijah felt in 1 Kings 19:5. God saw how tired Elijah was lying under that broom tree. The angel touched him and said, "Arise and eat, because the journey is too great for you."

God's Grace, Cafeteria-Style: I went upstairs to the cafeteria, through the line, and selected food items. I remembered that God had a special table prepared. As I sat down and bowed my head, a cafeteria worker who saw tears streaming down my face placed her hand on my shoulder and prayed. Although I came to receive physical nourishment, God knew I would not be able to eat, so He sent me spiritual food, speaking to me from Matthew 6:25, letting me know that life is more than food.

Final Test: When your loved one is on life support, the last words you want to hear are, "It's time to make a decision to disconnect the life support." The doctors performed the last test and found no brain activity.

Meeting of All the Great Minds

All of the specialists, social workers, and psychologists were there to present their final reports and to let me know I needed to make the decision to disconnect my husband's life support. I told them that only the Giver of Life could say when.

As I paused, God spoke to me in a still, small voice, saying, "Let him go because he belongs to Me, and My will must be done. I have allowed you to see that humans have done all that they can do, and now it is time for him to come home."

I then gave the doctors permission to disconnect man's life support and relinquished my husband to God's support. In those final moments, there was such a peaceful look on my husband's face.

What do you do when it's night, you are 1,500 miles away from home, and your husband has just died in a hospital room?

That still, small voice again whispers, "Peace, be still!" (Mark 4:39), and then you hear, "I will never leave you nor forsake you" (Hebrews 13:5). God had everyone in place to help me along the way. At the suggestion of a family member, I released my husband's body to a local funeral home.

Knowing how heavy my heart was, my husband's relatives had invited my sister and me to stay with them. Early the next morning I awoke suddenly, almost in a panic. *What am I going to do?* God's answer came immediately. "Call your Sunday school teacher, JC Frazier." It happens that he is also the owner of a funeral home.

When I called JC and shared with him what had happened, he said, "Put your sister on the phone." My sister told me that he said, "Don't let her think." When I thought about it later, it made sense: don't make any plans in haste.

JC coordinated everything by working with the funeral home in Texas. I was the recipient of the lesson he taught in Sunday school: "The eyes of the Lord are on the righteous, and His ears are open to their cry" (Psalm 34:15).

Part of God's final preparation was for me to go through my husband's illness and the planning of the final service, not for me but for my sister. My husband died on July 23, 1997. The following year, on July 24, 1998, my brother-in-law passed away. I did what God had prepared me to do. I went to the funeral home for the planning of his service.

Conclusion/Reflections

I now see God's purpose for my trials: to share my journey with others who have gone or are going through adversity, letting others know God will never forsake them.

I can now see the great I Am providing everything I needed. When I felt like I couldn't take another step, I received His supernatural strength. When I felt like I had cried my last tear, the great I Am spoke to me and said, *"I see your tears, but you must keep moving; the journey isn't over. Your mountaintop is near, for I will mend your broken heart and dry up every tear."*

God Will Have the Last Word

Each of us will go through our own season of adversity. We plant, we harvest, we laugh, we cry, we gain and lose some friends along the way. We each play our part upon the stage of life, and then we must take our bow at the curtain call and move to our eternal home.

Prepare to Leave the Mountaintop

You have dwelt long enough
at this mountain.
Deuteronomy 1:6

The top of the mountain is an oasis of pleasures, a place where an encounter with God can change your life. Peter, James, and John went with Jesus to the top of the mountain. It was during the experience of seeing Jesus, along with Moses and Elijah, and hearing God proclaim that Jesus was His Son, that brought everything into clarity and resulted in a life-changing experience.

I remember having a spiritual mountaintop experience in a Congress of Christian Education class. The instructor was Spirit-filled, anointed, and prepared me to face the giants in the valley. At the end of the last day of the class session, I arrived home to find out that thieves had broken into my home and taken some of my valuables. Unless you've had that experience, you can't imagine the feeling of being violated when you see your personal items strewn all over the floor. The shock of what had happened was unreal.

As I was picking up some of my items, the words of the Lord spoke to me from Matthew 6:19: "*Do not lay up for yourselves treasure on earth, where moth and rust destroy and where thieves break in and steal.*"

Meditating on this Scripture I realized that God would allow us to have mountaintop experiences to prepare us for the giants in the valley.

Because of the oasis of the mountaintop, Peter wanted to build a memorial. He wanted to hold on to the experience. But our mountaintop experiences prepare us for the giants in the valley. They are too powerful for us to handle on our own.

Remember God's words to Jehoshaphat in 2 Chronicles 20:15: *"For the battle is not yours, but God's.*"

God isn't standing on the sideline being an observer in your life; He's cheering you on with His Word!

God's Love on the Wings of a Dove

"So, I said, 'Oh, that I had wings like a dove! I would fly away and be at rest'" (Psalm 55:6). My mother and her friend loved to go fishing. They would leave home early in the morning and return late in the evening, always sharing their fish stories about the big one that got away.

I remember reading in the paper about a man who also loved to go fishing. One day, he left for his favorite fishing spot but never returned home. When the family received news that he was missing, they gathered at the site where he was last seen. They kept watch for six days and finally went home because the next day was Christmas.

One can only imagine the agony in their hearts as they reflected on the meaning of Christmas and remembered that Jesus came to a lost and dying world, bringing hope. Although a dark cloud of despair hung over their heads, they had hope in their hearts that their loved one would be found.

When they surrendered their will to God—Luke 22:42: "...*nevertheless, not My will, but Yours, be done*"—a dove, a symbol of God's love, came out of the water where their loved one had last been seen. God was speaking to the storm raging in their hearts: "*And He arose, and rebuked the wind, and said unto*

My Purple Hat

Chapter 3
God Uses the Insignificant to Accomplish the Impossible

*Now a certain woman named Lydia
Heard us. She was a seller of purple from the
city of Thyatira, who worshiped God. The
Lord opened her heart to heed the things
spoken by Paul.*
Acts 16:14

My Purple Hat

Aunt Octavia loved to wear her purple hat. The color purple represents wealth, royalty, and great status. I'm reminded of Lydia, who was a seller of purple. When Paul and his companions came to Lydia's city, she opened her home to them. Aunt Octavia wasn't rich materially, but her love for mankind made her spiritually rich. Like Lydia, she was the head of her household and generously shared with anyone in need.

Spirit of Laughter (Proverbs 17:22)

Aunt Octavia's laughter was contagious. When she laughed, the sparkle in her eyes captured the love in her heart. When she laughed, whatever load you were carrying would be lifted. Proverbs tells us, *"A cheerful heart is good medicine, providing healing and power."* Health centers agree with this Scripture, using laughter to treat some health problems, as laughter causes the body to release a chemical that brings about a state of relaxation, eases stress, and protects our hearts.

Bridge Builder

My aunt was a bridge builder. She lived out the fruit of the Spirit, starting with the fruit of love. Although she never owned an actual building, she helped rebuild lives by giving food to anyone in need, taking clothes off her back and giving them to another. She was a single parent, but she gave out of her limited income.

My sisters and I were the recipients of her sacrificial giving. Like the man in *The Bridge Builder*, she used her struggles and trials to build a bridge of love and compassion for future generations to cross.

When her health failed, Aunt Octavia had to go into a nursing home. Most days when I left work, I would visit her, always bringing a treat. On weekends, we would go up to the penthouse overlooking the lake, where we would enjoy the worship service and later have popcorn.

Elaine was Aunt Octavia's granddaughter and caregiver. I would watch Elaine tenderly stroke her grandmother's face, kiss her, and say with so much love, "Dear, dear, I will always be here for you."

Aunt Octavia's Last Request

One day when I went to visit Aunt Octavia, she told me she wanted a pair of tennis shoes. The first pair I purchased for her were too small, so I returned them. The second pair was a perfect fit. When I gave them to her, the glow on her face and twinkle in her eyes was confirmation as she said, "They are so-o beautiful and they are just right. No one will ever take them from me."

When I think about those shoes, to me that first pair represents our earthly shoes. When God calls us home, we will leave them behind. The second pair represents our heavenly shoes. The words to a song came to my mind: *I got shoes; you got shoes; all of*

God's children got shoes. When I get to heaven, gonna put on my shoes, gonna walk all over God's heaven."

Aunt Octavia won't be hard to find. She will be the only one wearing purple shoes.

On Friday evening, June 12, 1997, the doorway to Heaven opened and Aunt Octavia's name was softly called. As she entered through the doorway, a host of angels waited for her. One handed her a long, white robe, but another came forward to say, "I know white is traditional, but I have a purple one for you." When Aunt Octavia stepped through that doorway, she left her knee pain behind. Through that doorway, there was peace, love, joy, and freedom from pain.

Aunt Octavia, when I step through that same doorway, I know that I will see you. You won't be hard to find. You will be the only angel wearing purple, telling the others about the news of my arrival to the others.

Widows

And when he came to the gate of the city,
indeed, a widow was there gathering sticks.
—1 Kings 17:10

B ecoming a widow is an emotional, as well as a financial, devastation. The widow in the above Scripture lived in a society where widows were not only ignored but also went hungry. Unable to make ends meet, this widow decided to scrape the last bit of flour from her bin and pour the last drop of oil from the jar to make a final supper for herself and her son so they could eat it and die.

Suddenly a stranger called out to her, saying, "Bring me a drink and a piece of bread." She explained why she was gathering sticks.

The stranger explained who he was and said to her, "Do not fear; go and do as you said, but make me a small cake from it first, and bring it to me; and afterward make some for yourself and your son. For thus says the Lord God of Israel: 'The bin of flour shall not be used up, nor shall the jar of oil run dry, until the day the Lord sends rain on the earth'" (1Kings 17:13–14).

The reward for her obedience to Elijah, the prophet of God, was flour and oil that did not run out for many days.

God's provisions are still available to all widows. God's resources are always there, sometimes an unexpected check or a caring neighbor with a loaf of bread or a jar of oil. Widows in our churches today may need help. Social security checks will not cover the rising cost of living and the high cost of medication and medical bills. A widow's silent voice speaking to the church:

Jesus loves me, this I know; can you see
my needs when I come through the door?
How comfortable upon your cushion
pews you sit; did you ask if my needs are met?

From the corner of my eye, I see your
stare; Lord, do they even care?
Where I am now you soon may be; your
eyes will open and then you will see.
You ask His blessings on a selected few; I
wonder, Lord, did they mean me too?

Jesus Sees You When Your Back is Up Against the Wall

First Kings 19 gives details about the time that Elijah was running to save his life because of a threat from Jezebel. Like Elijah, there are times in our lives when we want to give up and say, "Lord, I can't take this anymore." The Lord knows when we have had enough and are physically, emotionally, and spiritually exhausted. Because the Lord is a God of order, He takes care of our needs in the order He knows is best rather than in the order we may think things should be done.

In Elijah's day, the Lord fed him physically, allowed him to rest for a while, and then said to him, *"Get up and eat some more; there is a long journey ahead."*

When our backs are against the wall and we want to give up, we should focus on God's words in

Matthew 3:16–17: "When He had been baptized, Jesus came up immediately from the water; and behold, the heavens were opened to Him, and He saw the Spirit of God descending like a dove and alighting upon Him. And suddenly a voice came from Heaven, saying, 'This is My beloved Son, in whom I am well pleased.'"

Jesus had authority, yet He was allowed to be tempted as we are so we would know that He knows what we are going through. The strength we need is shown in Matthew 4:10:"Then Jesus said to him, 'Away with you, Satan! For it is written, "You shall worship the Lord your God, and Him only you shall serve.'"

Our defense when we are tempted to give up is to remember 2 Corinthians 12:8–9: "Concerning this thing I pleaded with the Lord three times that it might depart from me. And He said to me, 'My grace is sufficient for you, for My strength is made perfect in weakness.'"

Jesus affirms in John 10:30: "I and My Father are one." Remember that the Good Shepherd is saying: Sometimes we find ourselves in a dark place that becomes our "cave." God knows when we've been in it long enough and need His light. Elijah had hidden in that dark cave long enough; God knew he needed to come out and receive His light.

What? No Salt?

My cousin passed away a few years ago, but I can still hear the frustration in her voice the day she was diagnosed with high blood pressure and diabetes. She stated, "When the doctor took away my salt, that was my daddy, but then on another visit he took away my sugar, and that was my mama."

However absurd that sounds, it speaks to the seriousness of the life-changing effects of a diagnosis. Some people have greater willpower than others. One woman who has diabetes said, "When I look at a piece of cake, I ask myself, Do I want that piece of cake or my foot? I then wiggle my toes and think I want my foot."

Many studies have shown the devastating effect that sugar and salt have on the body. According to an article in *Consumer Reports*, the average person consumes 150 pounds of sugar per year and about a ton of salt. That's hard to swallow.

In the Old Testament, we read about Lot's wife, who is not remembered for being a wife, mother, sister, or even a good neighbor, but only for being turned into a pillar of salt because she couldn't resist the urge to glance back. How often have we found ourselves looking back at our wrong choices or lost opportunities?

In the New Testament, Jesus tells us to remember that we are the salt of the earth, which describes how living the life of a Christian can bring balance and hope to a dying world as we season the lives of others with the love of Christ.

What's in Your Lunchbox?

There is a lad here who has five barley loaves
and two small fish.
John 6:9

In the above Scripture, the lad had only two fish and five barley loaves in his lunch, prepared by his mother just for him, yet he willingly gave them to Jesus, the real lunch-maker.

When I think about the lad in the text, I am reminded of Stanley, a second-grader in my sister's class. Every morning, Stanley brought shiny, colorful lunchbox to class, and he would place it on the table with all the other boxes. However, at lunchtime, Stanley would buy lunch in the cafeteria.

One day, Stanley announced that someday he was going to put lunch in his lunchbox. I see the faith of both lads. One had enough faith to give his lunch away, and the other had an empty lunchbox but lived-in faith that one day he would actually have lunch inside his box.

As Christians, sometimes our lives are like those lunchboxes, empty or with just enough for ourselves until we give them to Jesus, the master multiplier.

Prison of Isolation

Several passages in the Bible speak of lepers. A person with leprosy was forced to live in isolation away from family and friends.

Luke 8:43 speaks about a woman with an issue of blood who had spent all her living seeking a cure from physicians. Because of the rules of society, she had to isolate herself from the public. Desperate for a cure, she ignored society's rules for a chance to touch Jesus. She pressed her way through the crowd, extending her arm through an opening, her finger just touching the hem of His garment. Instantly, the warmth of healing went through her body.

Jesus didn't try to shame her but praised her for her courage. "Daughter, your faith has healed you. Go in peace and be freed from your suffering."

In 2014, there was an outbreak of Ebola, a very contagious disease. People who had contact with an infected person were required to go into isolation. There may have been some who kept their contact a secret for fear of being placed in isolation. In September of that year, it was reported that a nurse who treated a patient who had tested positive for the disease refused to be isolated, which would take her away from caring for patients who were in need. She was willing to break the rules of society.

Prayer

Lord, forgive us when our faith is weak. Many times, the challenges of life test our faith. Help us to know there is no victory without a sacrifice. We want the crown but not the thorns. Our healing will only come from sharing Your wounds.

Guilty

It was one of those mornings. A quote that I heard years ago came to live in my space: "The hurrier I go, the behinder I get." Nothing was moving out of my way. In fact, everything was getting in my way. I knew I was running late for work, so I decided I would drive a little faster, which meant I was exceeding the speed limit. I thought, *Just a couple more lights and I will be on the freeway.*

Suddenly, seemingly from out of nowhere, lights flashed. I pulled over to the side of the street. (*What do you do when you know you are guilty?*).

The officer said "Ma'am, you know you were going over the speed limit?"

My mind quickly and silently responded, Since he addressed you in such a respectful way, act in humility because you are guilty.

I said, "Sir, I know that I was speeding because I'm running late for work." That came from Proverbs 15:1: "A soft answer turns away wrath."

The officer's demeanor changed from professional to empathic. He asked, "Where do you work?" When I told him the name of the school, he said, "That's my old school," and then he inquired about some of his teachers. The conversation ended with, "You drive safely and have a good day"

I gently wiped the sweat from my brow. As I drove away, I thought, *I must visit the book of Proverbs more often. After all, it is a book of wisdom. Ask Him and He will give it to us.*

Chapter 4
Flowers Among the Rocks

Wings of Hope

I used the butterfly as a metaphor when I gave a reflection at a home-going service for a beloved friend. A butterfly is viewed as a symbol of hope. It dies as a caterpillar, is buried in a cocoon for a length of time, and emerges into a new life. It also needs sunlight to raise its body temperature in order to fly. When we transition from life to death, God's Son's light allows our bodies to be changed to eternal beings.

Rocks are placed in a butterfly garden to provide a resting place for the butterfly. Periodically, it will perch upon a rock with its face to the sun, and the body temperature rises, allowing it to fly.

On the afternoon following my friend's service, I was sitting on my patio reflecting on her legacy when the most colorful, beautiful butterfly came into my yard and floated majestically from flower to flower. I watched in awe, and suddenly it disappeared, as if to say, "Gaze upon my beauty only for a brief time."

Psalm 103:15 tells us that our mortal lives are like grass: they flourish like a flower of the field and soon fade away.

We were once like that clammy and repulsive caterpillar becoming a butterfly because we born into the ugliness of sin. When we accepted Jesus as our Savior, our transformation took place, allowing us to become His spiritual butterfly.

What? A Turkey Leg?

Recuperating from an injury I sustained on my way to church, I realized I would miss Communion the following Sunday. A few days later, I received a call from one of the deacons asking to come and give me Holy Communion. I gratefully accepted. They came, served communion, then gave me words of encouragement.

As they were leaving, a member from my church came to the door with a bag in her hand. She said, "I don't want to come in; I just want to give you this package."

I insisted that she come inside. The bag was still warm, and I couldn't wait to open it. There was a large smoked turkey leg inside. While eating, I reflected on her. She and I attend the same Sunday school class. Her spiritual presence and knowledge of God's Word speak to God's transforming power in her life. I thought about the meaning of her name, Dorothy, which is "a gift from God." *Ahh*, I thought, *no wonder this turkey leg is so good. It came from the one who is a gift from God.*

Our former pastor once gave an analogy about winning souls to Christ. Many ministers had visited a certain man, trying to get him to accept Christ. None of them were successful. One day, this old pastor went to visit him and brought him a pork chop. The pastor didn't talk to the man about Jesus like the other ministers did.

The following Sunday, the man came to church and gave his life to Christ. When he gave his testimony, he said, "I gave my life to Christ because of the pork chop. When the pastor came to visit, I was hungry, and he fed me. I saw Christ in him."

Caring for the earthly needs of a person is evidence of God's grace living within us, as stated in Matthew 25:35: *"For I was hungry, and you gave Me food; I was thirsty and you gave Me drink; I was a stranger, and you took Me in."*

When you give people food, they feel you truly care about them as individuals.

What a Friend

*Therefore, if there is any consolation in Christ,
if any comfort of love, if any fellowship of the
Spirit, if any affection and mercy, fulfill my
joy by being like-minded, having the same
love, being of one accord, of one mind. Let
nothing be done through selfish ambition
or conceit, but in lowliness of mind let each
esteem others better than himself. Let each of
you look out not only for his own interests,
but also, for the interests of others.*
Philippians 2:1–4

There are many kinds of friendships we encounter along life's way, but the uniqueness of one with a humble spirit will outlast them all.

In the school where I taught, my classroom had an adjoining door with another classroom. That door had never been opened until a unique teacher moved in and realized he could visit my room without having to go out into the hallway, if he could get that door open. He managed to open it, which started our bond.

Impressed by his tenacity, I soon discovered that he loved the Lord, his family (wife, daughter, and granddaughter), and had a passion for teaching. Anyone stopping by his classroom could readily see that he had high standards, values, and integrity, which he did all he could to relay to his students.

Over the years, we shared resources, equipment, ideas, joys, sorrows, and disappointments. Then one day, he informed me that he was being moved to another classroom upstairs. After his move, that adjoining door was closed again, but our friendship stayed the same.

Even though he retired a few years later, I still maintained a special relationship with him and his family. One day, his wife called to let me know he was in the hospital and could only have a limited number of visitors for about thirty minutes.

When I walked into his hospital room, the look on his face was priceless. He said, "Come on in! I'm so glad to see you!" He immediately began to inquire about my family and our coworkers. After about fifteen minutes, I told him I was going to leave since his wife had informed me that there was a time limit for him to have visitors. He insisted that I stay because he wasn't through talking. He stated, "Time is for other folks, but not you because we have so much to talk about."

As I looked around his room, all the flowers reminded me of what it must look like in Heaven's flower garden. He pointed out the flowerpot his granddaughter had made especially for him. She wrote on it how much she loved and appreciated all that he had done for her.

Later on, I mentioned to his granddaughter how proud her grandfather was of what she had written on that pot and that she had planted seeds of gratitude in his heart. With a smile, I told her it was up to her to make those seeds grow by fertilizing them with the love her grandfather had imparted to her. I encouraged her to allow God's Son to shine in her life, knowing that the harvest would be bountiful as she carried on the legacy of her grandfather.

As my mind replayed our teaching years, I remembered how I had often tried to slip past his door at the end of the day. When he saw me, he would tell me I was always in a hurry, then start telling me about his day. After a while, I would say, "I'm going home because I get to work early, and you are always late; you are never on time."

He said, "But I'm always here in time."

On June 3, Jesus said to my friend, "Your work on earth is done. You have fought a good fight; you've finished your course; well done, My good and faithful servant. It's time for you to rest from the work that you've done."

My friend packed up and moved upstairs. This time, he didn't have to force the door open. It was the door to Heaven that never closes yet opens but one way. Jesus welcomed him with a warm embrace. My friend smiled and said, "I now know I'm in time."

Bread!

The other day I was driving home and decided to take a different route. Traveling down a side street, I noticed the homes that had once been bright and vibrant were now worn and tattered from the wear and tear of the winters.

As I continued to travel, I reflected on the beautiful church I had just passed with its stained-glass windows. It was a beautiful brick building surrounded by neatly trimmed trees and grass. A tall tower extended above the roof. Various doors led toward the entrance. I marveled at the architectural craftsmanship. The main entrance had an arch with two large doors that had exquisite stained-glass windows topped with a cross. Many shades of taupe, gray, brown, orange, and green reflected the light.

As I continued driving down the street and came to a stoplight, I looked to my left and noticed the many rows of houses that were weatherworn from the harsh winters. Sandwiched between those houses was a church that had once been a store, now called a storefront church.

On the sidewalk in front of that church was a table covered with loaves of bread. As I wondered if anyone actually took the bread, a young man with a hood on his head approached the table. He looked around to see if anyone was watching, picked up a couple of loaves, placed them under his jacket, and disappeared around the corner. My thoughts went back to that large, beautiful church that was appealing to the physical eye, but there was no bread.

In John 6:48, Jesus is speaking about spiritual bread. He stated, *"I am the bread of life."* We must partake of Him each day to nourish our spiritual souls through His Word and prayer and allow the Holy Spirit to guide us.

At mealtimes, we give thanks and praise to God for our physical food that is temporary, but our spiritual food, His Word, is eternal. Someone once said, "We are all beggars telling someone else where to find food."

Your Bed is Always Ready

An elderly lady found herself all alone after her daughter married and moved to another state. She lived in the backwoods in the country. Her little dog was all she had to keep her company. Each night when she got into bed, the little dog would bark. The woman would toss and turn but was unable to sleep, thinking that someone was outside.

After many sleepless nights, she packed her small bag and made her way over to her friend's house. The friend, a member of her church, reminded the elderly woman that "your bed is always ready." The elderly woman could feel the love and knew she was always welcome.

As I reflected on this story, I looked at Matthew 25:35, where Jesus said, "For I was hungry, and you gave Me food; I was thirsty, and you gave Me drink; I was a stranger, and you took Me in." Jesus is saying that acts of kindness and charity done for someone else are done to Him as well.

The friend who always had the bed ready was my mom. I only found out about this story a few years ago when my sister shared it with me. I wasn't surprised, because that's the kind of person my mom is.

The Purpose of a Shoe

There are many different kinds of shoes. Some are for beauty only, especially the ones that are very high with pointed toes. Although you have five toes, only two or three will fit in that small space; the other ones will just hang out by themselves, pressing against the leather or other material, which will not be comfortable but will cause corns and sometimes blisters.

Some Christians are like those high heels, called stilettos. They become too high in their self-righteousness, and God has to allow them to fall so He can reach them through His Word. There is none righteous but the Father.

My sister walked out of church one Sunday, stepped down, and one of her heels broke off. At first, she tried to walk in that one heel; up and down she went. She finally gave up and took off the other shoe.

There are some Christians who are like that broken heel—broken for various reasons and still trying to walk until they become aware that God is saying, "Take off that other shoe and allow My Holy Spirit to give you balance."

Ruth 4:7–8 states, *"Now this was the custom in former times in Israel concerning redeeming and exchanging, to confirm anything: one man took off his sandal and gave it to the other, and this was a confirmation in Israel. Therefore, the close relative said to Boaz, 'Buy it for yourself.' So, he took off his sandal."*

My friend and I would always say, "One day we will find our Boaz," but we are confident in knowing this is symbolic of Christ redeeming us by shedding His blood for us on Calvary.

Chapter 5
The Fragrance of Praise

Let everything that has breath praise the Lord.
—Psalm 150, Verse 6

Singing Birds

A few days ago, I was talking to my sister who lives in the South. There was so much joy and excitement in her voice. She said, "When I woke up this morning and went into my den, there was a melodious sound coming from the fruit trees that Dad planted years ago. The trees are in full blossom, and there are different colors and sizes of birds. They moved from branch to branch, singing as if they were in concert. They sing day and night."

I soon found myself visualizing those birds. I could see those trees that our dad planted with so much love.

Although he is deceased, it's as if his spirit had been planted in the soil and absorbed by the roots, sent up through the trunk and into the branches so the birds could have a peaceful habitation that allows them to use the branches to sing their songs. As the wind of Dad's spirit breathes through the branches, each bird makes a musical sound in its own tune. Adjusting the lens of my imagination, I could see all the beautiful birds.

There was the warbler perched on the lower branch in the morning sun. His eyes were fixed on Heaven, his mouth was open, and his singing was so sweet as he sang, "There's a sweet, sweet spirit in this place."

I saw a chickadee perched on one of Mom's gladiolas. His song matched the pink bloom that started to peek from its shoot. The yellow warbler joined in the choir.

Over by the wire fence sat a bright red bird, looking as if he were posing for a photo shoot. By the trees, a robin was taking a bath in a water basin, flapping his wings as droplets flew through the air while he turned around and around.

Within earshot was a group forming a quartet, with unstoppable notes flowing from their throats. The melody that the hermit thrush made resonated in my ears, following our own musical scale, *Do-Re-Mi*.

Over to the side, the mockingbird was imitating all of the other sounds. My grandfather would say that in the springtime, the mockingbird would sing, "*Bobwhite, bobwhite, are your peas ripe?*"

The northern cardinal was among the most beautiful of all singers. The melody of the sparrow was so sweet. I'm sure the songwriter was inspired to write "*His Eye is on the Sparrow* after listening to him.

The peaceful killdeer's voice is far-reaching even after dark.

Sitting among the beautiful birds and their sweet chorus was a grumpy-looking bluebird. He seemed to have a frown on his face. As he moved in and out of the cavity of the stump of the tree feasting on insects, I was reminded of the Scripture on how God feeds the birds.

Suddenly his feathers ruffled, he lifted his head high, and there was a sparkle in his eyes. Then I saw Mrs. Bluebird. They immediately went to work building a nest. A few weeks later, blue eggs appeared, and later, baby birds. Papa Bluebird lost his frown and seemed to happily take his turn providing for his family.

How awesome is our Creator, placing musical notes within birds to offer up praise to Him! Psalm 150:6 says it all: *"Let everything that has breath praise the Lord. Praise the Lord!"*

*The four living creatures, each having six
wings were full of eyes around and within.
And they do not rest day or night, saying:
"Holy, holy, holy, Lord God Almighty, who
was and is and is to come!"*
Revelation 4:8

After a little girl was told about Heaven, how happy everyone will be, and that there will be singing to God day and night—*Holy, Holy, Holy*—she suddenly ran from the room, dashing past her sister.

"Where are you going?" asked her sister, the one who had told her all this.

The little girl replied, "I'm going to get my shoes. I want to be ready when it's time to go!"

Metaphorically speaking, every Christian is fitted with special shoes. These are fitted on our feet, shod with the gospel of peace and no fear of the devil. God promised to keep our feet firm, and when our feet slip, His mercy will uphold us (Psalm 94:18). We must wear our shoes at all times. When it's time to go, we won't have time to run to get them.

Mom's Lilies

Consider the lilies, how they grow: they
neither toil nor spin; and yet I say to you,
even Solomon in all his glory was not
arrayed like one of these. If then God so
clothes the grass, which today is in the
field and tomorrow is thrown into the
oven, how much more will He clothe you,
O you of little faith?
Luke 12:27–2

When my mom's lilies are in bloom, I look forward to arising early in the morning while the dew is still on their petals. It allows me to see how God has watered them. The garden is clothed in the array of God's beauty. I carefully choose the ones that are in full bloom to make a bouquet, arrange them in a vase, and place them on the table where Mom can admire their beauty.

Within a few days, they wither. As I replace them, I'm reminded of God's grace. Daily, we need our spirits to be refreshed by His Holy Spirit.

We are like the lilies that are planted in soil. They send down their roots seeking moisture and nourishment; so it is with our souls. God sends down His bountiful grace that revives our spirits with His love and mercy.

At times, the lilies in Mom's flower garden bend their heads down until the sun shines on them; so, it is with us. We need God's Son's light to speak to us from Psalm 24:9: *"Lift up your heads, O you gates! Lift up, you everlasting doors! And the King of glory shall come in."*

Potluck

Everyone brings a dish to a potluck dinner. When the table is set, there is something for everyone to feast on. In the city where I live, each year on Thanksgiving a special feast is given at a large hotel. Everyone is invited: the homeless, those who live in shelters, or those who just want a meal. All are welcome.

As we gather around our own tables with family and friends to share a meal, it is a place to reflect and connect. As we enjoy God's gift of grace, we have a glimpse of the banquet of the kingdom to come.

Jesus ate and drank with sinners. His kingdom was being revealed as He shared a meal. In Mark 2:15 He had dinner at Levi's house, where there were tax collectors and sinners sitting at the same table.

Matthew 22:2–10 talks about a king who held a marriage feast for his son and invited all of his special friends, but no one showed up. The king sent his servants out to the highways to invite both the good and the bad; no one was overlooked. No background checks were made, proper etiquette wasn't a prerequisite, and no dress code applied. Just come as you are.

Jesus extends a similar invitation in Matthew 11:28: *"Come to Me, all you who labor and are heavy laden, and I will give you rest."*

Shape Up

First Samuel 4:18 tells of the death of Eli after he received bad news from a messenger. Eli had not trained his two sons in the ways of the Lord, yet he allowed them to carry on in his place. When the messenger told him that his two sons had been killed and the ark of God had been captured, Eli fell over backward, broke his neck, and died, due to being old and heavy.

When I joined the YMCA, I thought about Eli after I saw so many overweight people in one place. Just maybe, had there been a YMCA in his day, Eli could have used the treadmill, bike, or other exercise equipment, and maybe he would not have died after the shocking news from the messenger.

Nutritionists warn us about the adverse effects of sodium, sweets, and fats on our health and stress the importance of eating more fruits and vegetables to stay physically healthy. While proper diet and nutrition can keep us physically healthy for a time, the ultimate diet is spirituality.

As 2 Corinthians 5:1 states, *"For we know that if our earthly house, this tent, is destroyed, we have a building from God, a house not made with hands, eternal in the heavens."*

Prayer

Lord, according to Your Word, my body is a temple. I must take care of it daily. That requires proper nutrition, exercise, and medical care. Most importantly, spiritual housecleaning.

Did You Say Clay?

And the vessel that he made of clay was marred in the hand of the potter; so, he made it again into another vessel, as it seemed good to the potter to make.
Jeremiah 18:4

Clay is unusable when it is brought from the field; it is hard and full of impurities. Therefore, it must be refined before it can be useful. Both hands must be used to shape a clay pot; the hands apply pressure to help shape and form the inside of the pot.

Our lives are shaped by the pressures of life. Sometimes the death of a loved one, an illness, or other calamities from the outside world help to strengthen the inner man. We give our brokenness to the Master Potter, and He will not cast us away but places us on His wheel as He alters our marred and broken vessels over and over again.

As in the reading of the cracked pot, our heavenly Father knows about our cracks as we continue to be obedient to His will. The seeds we sow will become flowers that will allow us to become a part of the Master's bouquet in His heavenly mansion above when our life journey is over.

Each day, the Lord will send new mercy just for that day, so we can say, *"Lord, I don't know what You have in store for my life today; Your hand I cannot trace. But every day I hear You say to me, 'Sufficient is My grace.'"*

Chapter 6
God Orchestrates Events to Fit His Plan

Let us lay aside every weight.
Hebrews 12:1

Heavy Luggage

I have not mastered the art of packing smart when I take a trip. I take out only two pieces of luggage but can't fit everything in that I need, so I end up with three pieces of luggage. What a relief it is when I actually have everything I need. First, I count the number of days I will be gone, and then I try to pack things I think I might need but somehow never wear.

When I arrive at the airport my luggage is weighed, and every time, an orange tag is attached that reads "overweight." This means I have to pay an extra fee in addition to my airfare.

I remember my sister telling me how my aunt has one piece of luggage and always has everything that she needs. She said the key is to roll your clothing. That was a good tip. I tried it but only ended up with more stuff. I have to consider the weather, and if it is winter, I have to have heavy coats and boots.

My friend always asks me the same question: "Are you packed yet?" She already knows the answer is no. I can never seem to pack in advance, and at the last minute, there is always something else I think I will need. So, I throw it in, adding to the weight.

First Thessalonians 4:17 is a Scripture that lets me know I won't have time to call the post office and have my mail held; the reservation number in my smart phone can't be retrieved; I must have advance reservations already made in Heaven; and there will be no need to pack.

My confirmation number is 111. One for the Father, one for the Son, and one for the Holy Ghost. There will be no extra charges. The price has already been paid by the precious blood of Jesus.

Bargain Hunters

*Come, buy, and eat. Yes, come, buy wine and
milk without money and without price.*
Isaiah 55:1

Some people will travel miles for a bargain. Department stores advertise sales on items that are "bargains" too good to pass up. These items have hidden costs that you usually don't find out about until you've made the purchase. They never tell you in bold print, "Not returnable." In haste to get the deal, the fine print isn't seen. The good deal is only for those who are selling. That makes sense. Why would anyone choose to save me money?

My aunt needed a TV, but she couldn't afford to buy a new one. Driving in her car one day, she saw a man on the street corner selling TVs. The deal was too good to pass up. She gladly gave the man the amount he was asking for. He told her that he would load it for her, and he placed it in a large box. When she arrived home, she asked her grandson to bring the box into the house. When her grandson returned, he told her the box was filled with rocks.

In the above Scripture, Isaiah's plea of *"wine and milk without money and without price"* sounds too good to be true, but it is true. Isaiah isn't making the offer; God is. The invitation is extended to everyone who has a spiritual thirst for the gospel blessings that can only be received by God's grace. You are a good candidate if you have no resources, no money, no power, or are empty and unfulfilled.

God can revive us from the valley. As we travel through our desert of barren land and our living conditions are hostile, His offer of water corresponds to His refreshment that restores our souls. He offers milk, the nourishment from His Word.

Then Abraham fell on his face and laughed, and said in his heart, "Shall a child be born to a man who is one hundred years old? And shall Sarah, who is ninety years old, bear a child?"
Genesis 17:17

Therefore, Sarah laughed within herself.
Genesis 18:12

God promised Abraham that he would become the father of many nations. This promise was fulfilled when Abraham was one hundred years old, and his wife, Sarah, was ninety.

Unlike the postal service, which guarantees delivery by a certain date for a fee, yet is at times not able to make that delivery due to circumstances beyond human control, we can find confidence in He brews 10:23: *"For He is faithful that promised."*

Scriptures that tell us to wait on the Lord can seem difficult to understand because we live in a society that is accustomed to instant gratification. Yet we find ourselves waiting for something almost every day.

There is a growing problem in the city where I live. People don't wait for the red light to change but just speed right through it without considering that they can cause harm to themselves and/or someone else.

One of the most challenging things to wait for is a test result. Be it an x-ray, ultrasound, or mammogram—to name a few—anxiety can creep in. To lessen anxiety's effect, we should remember that Paul admonishes us *"to not be anxious for anything,"* since that will not change the result of the test. We must use our waiting time to continue studying God's Word, meditating, and praying that He will help us keep in mind that He will fulfill His promises.

Luke 2 tells us that Simeon waited for the promise that he would not see death until he had seen the Messiah. Being a just and devout man, he had learned to cling to the promises of the Holy Spirit even though he was in his old age.

God's Promise

God didn't promise us all sunshine in our lives, but He did promise He would speak peace into our storms. He didn't promise that we would not have to go through the valley to get to the mountaintop, but He did promise to guide us through life's ups and downs. Though the billows may roll above our heads, He promised he wouldn't let us drown.

He promised rest for the weary, that He would bear our load, because He knows what's down the road.

He promised we wouldn't be tempted beyond what we could bear. He will always provide a way out of the tempter's snare.

He promised victory to those who faint not, for He is waiting, waiting around the bend. The crown of life is ours when we make it to the end.

Regift the Gift

When people receive gifts they don't want or cannot use, they pass them on. This practice is called "regifting." I gave a graduate a gift that I had carefully selected and felt good about. However, I admit I felt disappointed when I was never thanked. I overheard her mother tell someone how she regifted things she couldn't use.

I thought, *Maybe that's what happened to the gift that I gave her daughter.*

How often have we taken the time to say, "Thank You, Lord, for the gift of each brand-new day?" Lamentations 3:22–23 speaks about the Lord's mercies and compassions that are new every morning: *"Great is thy faithfulness."* Each day is a new opportunity to regift the love of Jesus.

Regift the light of God's love, full of mercy and compassion from heaven above. The gift of His sacrifice so brilliantly shines, that we may be filled with redemption divine. With purity and truth, He guides us through each brand-new day to witness to others along the way. When you receive Him, He will open up the eyes of your heart, filling it with joy that never departs. He speaks in a still voice that we can hear, bidding us to come without fear.

The Lord showers His gifts upon you to encourage others who don't know what to do. Show kindness each day and make His presence known.

Regifting is the way that His love lives on. Psalm 118:24: *"This is the day the Lord has made; we will rejoice and be glad in it."*

Prayer

Great is Thy faithfulness.
Lamentations 3:23

*Lord, thank You for the gift of this
brand-new day. It is a new bank account
of grace and mercy that I can draw from,
knowing You are greater than any problem,
calamity, or challenge that lies before me this
day. Help me to regift Your love to others.*

Flying First Class

I frequently fly to visit my family who live in the South. I am content flying second-class, but I thought about the advantages for those who fly first-class. I know they get served first, since I can see this through the opening in the curtain that separates us, and I know they also pay a higher fare.

The second-class section provides ample leg room and a choice of peanuts or pretzels, along with a small cup of soda or water, for snacking if desired.

On one of my trips home, I remember that the sky was clear and the flight was going great until I arrived in Atlanta, where I had to change planes.

The weather worsened and there came a downpour. When I arrived in Meridian and went to claim my luggage, I was told that it was not on the plane. The airline took my information and said they would deliver my luggage once they received it.

When it finally arrived at my house, I discovered that my clothes were wet, some beyond repair. I thought about the people who flew first-class and wondered if the airline labeled their luggage in a special way so it wouldn't be left out in the rain.

When I read Hebrews 10:19— *"Therefore, brethren, having boldness to enter the Holiest by the blood of Jesus"*—I thought about how the curtain in the temple separated the people from entering the holiest of holy places. Only the priest could enter.

In Matthew 27:51, the veil of the temple was rent from top to bottom, giving access to everyone. We are all first-class Christians; Christ died for all. I don't have to wonder what's going on behind the curtain.

However, I still think about those who fly first-class. Are they really different? Better than I? We all ascend and descend at the same time. All of us have to follow the same rules, and none of us can walk when the seatbelt sign is on. If the plane crashes, God forbid, we will all go down together.

A few weeks ago, a news headline caught my attention: "Passenger dragged from plane due to overbooking, the passenger refused to give up his seat."

As Christians, we don't have to worry about our seats. We've already received our flight plans that have been sealed by the blood of Jesus. When our names are called, we will have a direct flight to Heaven, with Jesus as our pilot. We don't have to worry about turbulence. There will be clear skies and smooth sailing all the way to that holy city! And no lost luggage.

Thank you, Lord. You paid my fare. I'm now a first-class Christian rider all the way to heaven.

Joy in the Clay

*Then I went down to the potter's house,
and there he was, making something at the
wheel. And the vessel that he made of clay
was marred in the hand of the potter; so
he made it again into another vessel, as it
seemed good to the potter to make.*
Jeremiah 18:3-4

Today, I picked up a piece of clay. As it started to crumble and I looked at those small pieces in my hand, it opened up a little treasure box in my memory labeled, *Courage, Faith, and Perseverance.* The contents within simply said *"Joy,"* and that allowed me to go back to a scene that played out in my class-room setting.

As I stood outside my door greeting the usual mixture of freshman personalities, one girl stood out from all of the others. There was something about her inner beauty that went beyond her face. It was as if I could see the light within her heart.

As I checked the attendance and noticed her name, which means "Great Joy," I was reminded that names can give a glimpse into the inner person. As time went on, I could see that she was very focused on her goals to graduate from high school and attend college.

During her freshman year, she tried out for the basketball team. During the physical, it was discovered that she had a lump in her lower leg, which turned out to be cancer.

After completing chemo, she returned to school. That smile was still there! She had a greater determination to reach her goals than before. Everyone was inspired by her strength, faith, courage, and perseverance.

Just when we thought everything was going well, her annual checkup revealed that the cancer had spread. It was determined that her best chance for survival was to amputate her leg below the knee. When I spoke to her grandmother to inquire about her progress, she stated, "Oh she is getting ready to come back to school."

When the young woman returned to school on crutches, there was no self-pity, only a greater focus and determination. Even though she had to stop by the bathroom to change her bandages, she was never late for class.

One day she came to class and handed me a piece of paper with a poem she had written entitled *Making It on Broken Pieces*. In the poem, she talked about how her life had been broken into pieces, but with faith in God, she would pick-up her life piece by piece and use the pieces to build a bridge on which she would travel to fulfill her goals.

She graduated from high school and entered college but passed away during her freshman year. God's purpose for her life had been fulfilled.

I'm reminded of how the Master Potter spoke to Jeremiah as He said, *"Arise and go down to the potter's house."* She was placed on the potter's wheel and each broken piece of her life was mended in preparation for her heavenly home. She fought the fight and finished her course.

Because she endured the pressure,
Like the lump of clay,
She is now a part of God's heavenly bouquet.

When you are broken, and you don't
know what to do,
Stop by the Potter's House,
there is healing just for you!!

For Notes

Chapter 7
Faith Moves the Soul Beyond What the Eyes Can See

Though He slay me, yet will I trust Him.
Job 13:15

Look Upward Through Tragedy

My friend is the epitome of a Christian with unwavering faith who has the special gift of encouragement. In spite of her many tragedies and the loss of loved ones, she unselfishly helps and encourages others. Even with her own health challenges and a daughter who is ill, she reaches across the miles every week to call my mother, who is 900 miles away. They sing, pray, and encourage each other in the Lord.

I'm in awe of how she forms friendships. She shared with me how she met a lady at the hospital who had just received news that her father, who lived out of town, had passed. The lady was in great distress because she was taking care of an ill daughter, so she could not leave to attend her father's funeral. My friend told the lady to go home and pack her clothes for the funeral, as she would step in to care for her daughter. My friend said, "She allowed me to take care of her daughter, and I had just met her. Of course, I was true to my word. I was at the hospital every day, tending to her daughter."

Their friendship continued over the years. When the lady's daughter passed, my friend was right there for spiritual support.

A few years later, she received a hysterical phone call from that same mother early in the morning. The mother stated, "What am I going to do? My son has killed his own son."

My friend didn't have any words to console her. She simply said, "Let's pray," because she knew that as we pray, "*the Spirit makes intercession for us with groanings which cannot be uttered*" (Romans 8:26–27).

The Teapot Story (Don't Give Up—Don't Quit)

One afternoon, an elderly couple entered a lovely tea shop. A busy waiter directed them with a wave of his hand to sit at a table in the far corner. On the table was a beautiful teapot surrounded by delicious-looking scones, sandwiches, and cookies.

The man started to turn to go back to the counter to explain they didn't have enough money for such a feast, when the teapot began to speak. "Please sit down and do not be afraid. My Master wishes you to be His guest. Take and eat whatever suits you while I tell you a story." Startled but curious, the couple sat down to listen to the teapot's story.

"You see, there was a time when I was just an old hard, gray lump of clay. I was very sad because I felt so useless. One day, a Master Potter came along and picked me up. He began to pat, twist, turn, and re- shape me. It really hurt, so I asked Him to please stop, but He simply looked at me with a kind smile and said, 'Not yet.'"

As the teapot spoke, it poured out tea for the couple into delicate cups that never emptied or grew cold.

The teapot seemed to glow and light the dark corner like a lamp as it continued its story.

"Next, He put me on this wheel and began to spin me around. I got so dizzy I couldn't even see where I was going, and I began to feel ill. I begged Him, "Please let me off!" He replied, 'Not yet.'

"The worst was yet to come. However, my Master then put me into the oven. It was so incredibly hot that I cried out, but all He said was, 'Not yet.'

"Finally, the oven door opened. He took me out and set me on the table. I thought, *Whew! Thank goodness that is over!* But then He began to paint me with this awful-smelling stuff. I could hardly breathe when He put me back into the oven for a second time. It was even hotter than before! I thought I would die for sure. Just when I was ready to give up, He gently lifted me from the oven.

"After a long rest, my Master came by and picked me up. I could see my reflection in His eyes and saw that I had been transformed. I was now beautiful. He told me that it was my reward for being so patient and strong. I asked Him how I could repay Him, and His face lit up.

"My Master, Jesus Christ, then explained my purpose to me: 'Pour out your story to everyone you meet. Don't be discouraged if they don't hear or understand you. Keep your lid open a crack so I may fill you with My Spirit wherever you may be. I will guide you all the rest of your days.'"

The teapot seemed to glow even brighter as it finished sharing, "It is such an honor to serve my Master that I have been filled with joy ever since!"

The couple had tears in their eyes when the teapot finished its tale. They promised to share His story with others and come to visit.

This delighted the teapot even more. He knew his Master would be pleased because he was serving His purpose.

(Author unknown. Used with permission from The Tea Shelf: https://theteashelf.com/the-teapot-story/)

Blessed be the God and Father of our Lord Jesus Christ, the Father of mercies and God of all comfort, who comforts us in all our tribulation, that we may be able to comfort those who are in any trouble, with the comfort with which we ourselves are comforted by God.
2 Corinthians 1:3–4)

For we are His workmanship, created in Christ Jesus for good works, which God prepared beforehand that we should walk in them.
Ephesians 2:10

A Child's Cry

Growing up, I was intrigued by elderly people's stories. One day, I was having a conversation with an elderly Christian woman. She told me how God had brought her family through many hardships. She stated, "Although by many people's standards we were poor, we were spiritually rich because we always kept God at the center of our lives."

She continued to tell me that she, her husband, and their eighteen-month-old baby girl lived on a farm. She said "Yes, the work was very hard, but we raised our own food and had plenty to eat during the winter months."

With pride in her voice, she said, "My baby was so good. She never cried and always slept through the night, until one cold winter night when her scream awakened us. Frantically, we ran to her room. As I entered the room, I saw that she was okay, but through the window, we could see flames shooting up in the air from our barn where we kept our animals and stored food for the winter. All of the animals were killed. We lost everything and later found out that someone had deliberately set fire to our barn."

I asked, "What did you do?"

She said, "We thanked and praised God for the child's cry, because the barn was very close to our house."

I then asked, "What do you do when you lose everything?

She said, "But child, we didn't lose everything. We still had our family and the love of God in our hearts."

When Satan tries to plant fear in my mind, I turn to Isaiah 41:10: "Fear not, for I *am* with you; be not dismayed, for I *am* your God. I will strengthen you, yes, I will help you, I will uphold you with My righteous right hand."

What is Your Name?

Now the Lord came and stood and
called as at other times, "Samuel! Samuel!"
And Samuel answered,
"Speak, for Your servant hears."
1 Samuel 3:10

Parents choose their children's names for various reasons—after a relative or famous people, or because they sound pretty.

A teacher had to carry one of kindergarteners to the office to call her mother. The child's name was missing from the contact card. When the principal asked, "What do they call you at home?" she said, "Sister Girl."

In biblical times, God gave His people names that spoke of their significance and purpose. In Genesis 17:5, Abram's name was changed to Abraham to become the father of many nations. Sari's name was changed to Sarah (her name means princess); Isaac's name means laughs. In Genesis 21:6 Sarah said, "God has made me laugh." Hannah's name means graciousness or favor. She named her son Samuel (its Hebrew meaning "ask of God" or "heard by God").

I remember a young couple eagerly awaiting the arrival of their first child. The mother died giving birth, and I don't know if she named the little girl. Rachel (Genesis 35:17–18) gave birth in great pain and knew she was going to die, so she named her son Benoni, (son of trouble). Jacob renamed him Benjamin (son of my right hand).

As stated in Isaiah 43:1, we know that the Lord calls by name those who belong to Him, even if it is "Sister Girl."

Chapter 8
A Smile from Heaven

Baby in a Basket

When I read the headline "Newborn Baby Found in a Clothes Basket, Wrapped in a Blanket in the Hallway of a Church," my mind went back to a baby who was found in a basket floating in the Nile River. I thought about Moses's mother and the mother of the abandoned baby. Both mothers could have shared something in common: joy and fear, but I thought about the two baskets. One was a laundry basket, perhaps plastic, while the other was handmade with love and care.

In biblical times, baskets were made from plant materials: leaves, stalks, and twigs. One can only imagine the love that Moses's mother poured into making his basket as she coated it with papyrus and tar to make it waterproof. By faith, she placed him in the Nile River, not knowing the Divine plan that God had for her son. She only knew that her faith in God allowed her to let him go and allow God to fulfill His plan for Moses's life.

God can use any ordinary basket as a vessel to bring about something extraordinary for His glory.

God the Master Photographer

Train up a child in the way he should go,
and when he is old, he will not depart from it.
Proverbs 22:6

A little girl was walking home from school, which was only a short distance. As she walked along, it started to rain. Suddenly the lightning flashed, and the thunder rolled as a jagged bolt of lightning ripped across the sky.

Meanwhile, Mom was panicking, as she knew her child was walking home from school. She ran down the road, thinking how frightened her child must be. Drawing near, she was amazed at the radiance on her child's face, and she asked her, "Were you afraid?"

"No, Mom," said her daughter. "It was so much fun. God took my picture all the way home."

Remember, when you train up your children, in dire situations they will see the photographer and not just the images.

Little Mite

And He saw also a certain poor widow
putting in two mites.
Luke 21:2

My friend Bessie was visiting her family, who lived in another state. On Sunday, she attended church. Sitting in the pew, she noticed that the man sitting beside her had a childlike spirit. She introduced herself and asked what his name was. They then started a conversation.

Bessie has an outgoing personality and never meets a stranger. She reminds me of Proverbs 18:24: *"A man who has friends must himself be friendly."*

When it was time for the offering, she asked the man if he would like her to fill out his offering envelope. He gladly accepted. She told him, "Now, you don't have to tell me how much you want to put in for your tithe."

He proudly proclaimed, "One dollar."

As I thought about this young man's offering, I was reminded of the widow's mite in Luke 21:1–4, which speaks of Jesus sitting opposite the place where people were putting their offerings into the temple treasury. Many rich people put in large amounts, but a poor widow put in two small copper coins worth only a few cents.

Jesus told His disciples that she gave more than all the others because she had given out of her poverty. God saw the cheerfulness of the young man and the willingness of the widow to give all that they had and received them as a sweet smell.

My New Friend

Thank you, my new friend, for listening
with your heart.
God is well pleased because you did your part.
We met as strangers, but you soon became my friend.
You opened up your heart, and I walked right in.
God is pleased with the way you put my heart at ease.

If by chance our paths should cross again, my heart will welcome you to come on in. Your welcoming spirit was filled with love; I know you were sent from Heaven above.

Childlike Faith

The term "childlike faith" isn't found in the Bible, but its concept can be found in several passages. When Jesus's disciples wanted to know the greatest in the kingdom, Jesus called a little child, set him in the midst of them, and then explained that having an attitude of a child is essential to enter the kingdom of Heaven.

He said, "Assuredly, I say to you, unless you are converted and become as little children, you will by no means enter the kingdom of heaven" (Matthew 18:2–3).

A four-year-old was in class one day when a lesson being taught reminded her about the story of Jonah that she had learned in Sunday school. She became very excited and asked the teacher, "Did you know that Jonah was swallowed by a whale and stayed in his stomach for a very long time before the whale spit him out?"

Not a believer, the teacher explained why that was not scientifically possible because of the structure of the whale's stomach and throat.

The little girl wasn't convinced by what the teacher said, and with continued excitement, replied, "When I get to heaven, I'll ask Jesus!" (Jonah 1:17; 2:10)

Teach Them to Pray

For this cause everyone who is godly
shall pray to You in a time when
You may be found; surely in a flood of great waters
they shall not come near him.
Psalm 32:6

I had a conversation with a mom about prayer. She indicated that she had taught her child how to pray at an early age. They prayed together each night. With a smile on her face, this mom told me how they continued to talk every day, even when her daughter went off to college many miles away. When they would talk at night, her daughter always said, "Mom, don't forget to say your prayers!"

My sister, who lived far away, was going to have surgery. The night before, I heard my mom talking in her bedroom. I immediately rushed to her door because I thought she was calling for help. But then I realized she was talking to God, praying for my sister. I thought about the words in the song *I Pray We'll All Be Ready*, with special emphasis on *"You need to learn how to pray; you can't rely on Mother's prayer when she is gone."*

Reflection

Prayer transcends space and time. The most valuable lesson you can teach your children is how to pray. Prayer directed to God goes to Him without delay. The airline may misdirect your luggage and your flight might be diverted to another airport, but this is never the case with God.

You Can't Take It Back!

The teacher glanced at the clock in her classroom and thought, *Thank God it's almost break time.* The children in her second-grade class were unusually active, especially Tim, who had been acting up all morning and had ignored all of her warnings to send him to time-out. She thought, *It has to be a full moon.*

At that very moment, Tim dashed across the room and knocked over another student's desk. He had tested her last nerve, the one that's in reserve.

She yelled out to him, "Didn't I tell you to sit your hardheaded self down?"

Sitting down and looking dejected, Tim said, "You hurt my feelings."

She immediately said, "I'm sorry."

"That didn't take it away," he replied. "My feelings are still hurting."

It may seem hard to forgive when our feelings and pride have been hurt. You might think that the person who wronged you might not deserve forgiveness, but we don't deserve God's forgiveness. He commands us to forgive because it brings freedom even though it hurts.

Some Scriptures to read about hurtful words: Proverbs 12:18; 15:1; 15:4; 16:24; 19:4; and 21:23; Psalm; 34:13; Matthew 6:14; James 3:5; and Ephesians 4:29.

Sunset

The Mighty One, God the Lord,
has spoken and called the earth
from the rising of the sun
to its going down.
Psalm 50:1

Have you ever stood in awe as you watched a sunset? It is the majestic voice of God speaking at the close of the day. He pulls the curtain of light as He ushers in the night, allowing us to set aside all of our cares and worries, even our missed opportunities to show His love to others. With every new sunset we can release our dashed hopes, wounded spirits, broken hearts, and regrets.

O Lord, our Lord, how excellent is Your name
in all the earth, who have set Your glory
above the heavens!
Psalm 8:1

If the heavens that You created declare Your glory; should not my praise shine as brilliantly as the sunset?

You Smell Like the Rose of Sharon

But the Lord said to him,
"Go, for he is a chosen vessel of Mine."
Acts 9:15

Chosen Vessel

One day, the Lord was looking for a vessel He could use. Would it be like the woman at the well found in John 4:1–42? Jesus told this woman that He had water that would take away her thirst forever. This was not water that was two parts hydrogen and one-part oxygen, but spiritual water that would satisfy thirst forever.

Are you thirsty? Is there a void in your life that you can't seem to fill? Tried everything? Try Jesus and you will never thirst again. John 4:13: "Jesus answered and said to her, 'Whoever drinks of this water will thirst again, but whoever drinks of the water that I shall give him will never thirst. But the water that I shall give him will become in him a fountain of water springing up into everlasting life.'"

Whatever your sin, an encounter with Jesus will allow you to drop your water pot filled with guilt and shame. Jesus will make you into a brand-new vessel for His service.

What is that Exquisite Fragrance?

Now thanks be to God who always leads us in tri-
umph in Christ, and through us diffuses the fragrance
of His knowledge in every place. For we are to God the
fragrance of Christ among those who are being saved
and among those who are perishing.
2 Corinthians 2:14–15

This passage tells us that, as Christians, we should have a distinctive aroma. How often have you heard someone ask, "What is that fragrance you're wearing?"

This reminds me of an allegory about a row of chamomile flowers that were planted beside a gravel walkway. The walkway said to the flowers, "You smell delightfully fragrant today; tell me why."

The flowers replied, "We've been walked on a lot today, and the more we are crushed, the more fragrant we become. That's our nature. However, the more you are walked on, the harder you become."

When Christians are pressed with sorrow and trials, the indwelling Holy Spirit allows us to become more fragrant. God will allow our lives to be touched by sorrow so that we may feel someone else's pain. Like the petals of a rose crushed to allow the sweet perfume to flow, our compassion can flow into someone's life, allowing them to smell the fragrance of Christ.

In the Old Testament, perfume-makers made special oils used only for anointing holy things. In Luke 7:38, one can only imagine the intensity of the oil that Mary poured on Jesus, permeating the room. If you were to walk into a room and someone said, "You smell like the oil from Mary's alabaster jar," like me, you would be in total awe!

Finish the Race: Winter Olympics 2016

The newspaper headline read: "Women's 4 x 100 Relay Team. The Baton Was Dropped after Another Member Collided with Another Runner."

After reading that headline, my mind replayed the tapes in my head. I had watched that relay team all during the Winter Olympics and was watching when another runner collided with the runner as the baton was being passed to the final runner, causing her to drop the baton. There was disbelief, horror, and frustration on the runner's face. I watched as she retrieved the baton and continued to run to the finish line.

When the captain was asked why they continued to run when they knew they were disqualified, she stated, "We had to finish the race."

They appealed their case to the Olympic Committee and were allowed to rerun the race. The replay of the tape showed that another runner had stepped over into our runner's lane, causing her to trip. This was a violation. This technicality allowed them to run the race over, and this time they won.

As Christians, how often have things in our lives been running smoothly when Satan steps into our lane, causing us to fall? We must apply Proverbs 24:16 to our lives: *"For a righteous man may fall seven times and rise again."*

Our spiritual life is like a race each Christian must run. At some point, we must stop walking or jogging and start running. When we fall down, we can appeal our case to the Righteous Judge (God). Paul wrote these strong words to the believers in Galatia: *"You were running a good race. Who cut in on you to keep you from obeying the truth?"*

We must run with a purpose, like Paul, who was coming to the end of his life's journey. He stated, *"I have fought a good fight, I ran my race and finished my course"* (2 Timothy 4:7).

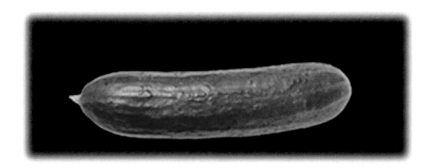

Cool

"Look!" he answered, "I see four men loose,
walking in the midst of the fire;
and they are not hurt."
Daniel 3:25

Have you heard the phrase "cool as a cucumber"? It is said that a cucumber exposed to extreme heat can remain ten degrees cooler on the inside than on the outside.

How can Christians remain cool on the inside when everything around them is falling apart, when everything they have labored for has been destroyed?

I took a drug education class, and my instructor wanted to impress upon us the impact of drug use on the lives of others. He gave each of us some modeling clay and told us to build our dream house and family. After working on that for about an hour, we were asked to move to another person's work. He told us to destroy everything and rebuild. The emotions were extremely high as we watched the beautiful homes and our families destroyed. The instructor's assignment made an impact on each of us.

As Christians, how do we handle it when our world has been turned upside down? It may be the sudden loss of a loved one, the destruction of families due to drugs, or the killing of innocent children.

How do you remain cool on the inside when you've been placed in the furnace of adversity? We remain cool like the Hebrew boys in Daniel 3 because Jesus is our center.

Prayer

Dear Lord, enroll me in Your school.
When placed on my wheel of adversity,
keep my center cool.
You are my fortress;
I place my trust in You.
You cover me under Your wings
of protection when I don't know what to do.
Lord, I am empowered through
my relationship with You.
In my furnace of affliction,
I trust You to see me through.

The Jesus Touch

Be cleansed.
Matthew 8:3

When I was teaching, I invited a young man to come speak to my students about AIDS. He told me, "I have full-blown AIDS." This was a time when people were not as educated about the virus as they are today. Lack of knowledge creates fear.

On the day of the presentation, my guest arrived early and asked me not to tell the students that he had AIDS. I concurred. He stood by the door and shook each student's hand as he or she entered the room. After they were all seated, he introduced himself and stated that he had AIDS. None of the students appeared frightened or alarmed.

I smiled with amazement at my students and my guest as we were moving forward in dispelling myths about how you can and cannot get AIDS. The students were very interested in his story. He shared with them how lonely he became when his family disowned him, until he found a support group.

I thought about those who had leprosy during Jesus's ministry. They had to live outside of their communities and became very lonely. Their support group was each other, as evidenced in Luke 17:13–14 where Jesus encountered ten lepers. "And they lifted up their voices and said, 'Jesus, Master, have mercy on us!'

So, when He saw them, He said to them, 'Go, show yourselves to the priests.' And so, it was that as they went, they were cleansed."

Jesus gave His life for us. His blood healed us from sin, a disease worse than AIDS or leprosy. All we have to do is trust in His Word.

Teach Them to Pray

For this cause everyone who is godly
shall pray to You in a time when
You may be found; surely in a flood of great waters
they shall not come near him.
Psalm 32:6

About the Author

Willie E. Burge Robinson was born in Meridian, Mississippi, the youngest of three girls. Their parents instilled the love of Christ, honesty, and hard-work ethics into the lives of their children. God has always been at the center. They attended church every Sunday and were involved in many church activities. Willie's passion was always drama. She was accustomed to getting the lead role in plays. In addition, she has been honored with the following awards:

- The Bearman's Outstanding Teacher's Award
- Who's Who Among America's Teachers
- McDonald's Golden Apple Excellence Award
- MMABSE Outstanding Teacher Award

Having a great desire to serve the community as well, she accomplished the following:

- Gospel Choir Advisor
- Coordinated School's City-wide Personal Hygiene Drive for United Way

- Collaborated with the City Health Department securing speakers to bring awareness of AIDS to the community
- Worked with the Milwaukee Police Department Drug Education Unit providing resources to the community
- Volunteered for Salvation Army
- Membership & Program Director with the YMCA

She joined Pilgrim Rest Missionary Baptist Church, where she served in various ministries, including president of a mission circle, a member of the gospel choir, Sunday school, and Bible class.

In 1997, her husband died unexpectedly while on vacation in Houston, Texas. Through this journey of testing, she was the recipient of God's grace. He placed people in her path every step of the way; she felt that she truly was a stranger in a foreign land.

As she looked back over her life, she felt a great desire to set her focus on putting encouraging words in writing so that they would be available to people nationwide.